This book belongs to

_____

你行的
nǐ xíng de
You can do it!

Let's Learn Chinese.
It's so much **FUN!**

Dear Parent and Educator,

Chinese For Kids Learning Fun Workbook is a supplement to introduce Chinese language plus culture in the classroom and at home. This workbook is a tool for children to learn and practice Chinese at their own pace. Use your favorite pencils, colored pencils and crayons to complete fun learning activities.

Features include real images, colorful kid-friendly layouts and parent friendly explanations. Get your child excited to learn Chinese with fun culture facts, puzzles and activities. The goal of Chinese For Kids workbooks is to help children stay motivated while giving them the confidence they need to learn Chinese in school and at home. Thank you for letting us join your language learning journey.

- Chinese For Kids Workbooks

Copyright © 2021 by Queenie Law
ISBN: 9798459560671
Chinese For Kids Learning FUN Workbook Ages 5+

Special thanks to the Zeng family and our beta readers.

Disclaimer
The publisher and author disclaim responsibility for any loss, injury, or damages caused as a result of any instructions described in this book.

1 Learn about the Chinese language.

5 Make new friends.

6 Secret Message

13 Pretend to be the teacher.

14 Flower Maze

谢谢。
Xiè xiè
Thank you.

Thank you

21 Be Kind.

23 Word Search

Parents and educators check out more learning resources

 www.adoreneko.com

Instagram @adorenekobooks

Learn Chinese

The Chinese language is spoken all over the world. There are many different forms of Chinese. Mandarin is a form of Chinese with the most speakers (more than 1 billion).

China
Taiwan
Singapore

中文
Zhōng wén
Chinese language

Mandarin is the official language of China (People's Republic of China), Taiwan and one of Singapore's national languages.

Write the language(s) you can speak below.

What do you see?

You may see some Chinese characters that look like their meanings, while others may not. The Chinese language does not have an alphabet. Practice reading and writing Chinese to remember the characters.

Look at the Chinese character for mountain 山 (shān).

Mountain

Shān
Mountain

Color the Chinese character for mountain.

Make Your Own

Some Chinese characters are based on pictographs. Pictographs are symbols that represent a word or phrase.

Try This!
Draw a picture. Make your own symbol for that picture.

Simplified and Traditional Chinese

China and Singapore use the simplified form of written Chinese. Taiwan uses the traditional form. In simplified Chinese, some characters will have less strokes than the same ones in traditional. We will be writing simplified Chinese in this workbook.

Writing Strokes

Chinese characters are written with strokes.
In this workbook, numbered strokes will guide your writing.

Let's look at some strokes.

Follow the numbers to trace the strokes.

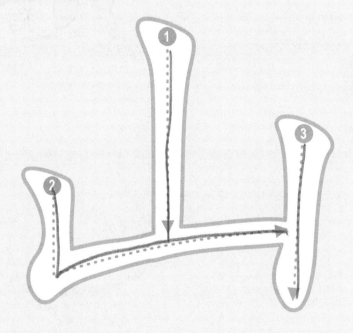

山
Shān
Mountain

干得好
gàn dé hǎo
Well done!

Trace and write.

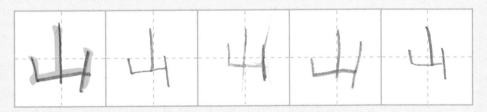

Greetings!

Introduce yourself to make new friends.

你好!
Nǐ hǎo
Hello!

你叫什么名字?
Nǐ jiào shén me míng zì?
What is your name?

Write your name.

HELLO
my name is
猫 Cat Mão

我叫
Wǒ jiào
My name is

Claudia
Kim

Draw a picture of yourself.

老师 好!
Lǎo shī hǎo!
Hello teacher!

Try This!
To greet their teacher, students in China stand up and shout
老师 好!

Secret Message

Find and color the Chinese words to reveal a secret message.

同学	再见	老师	好
Tóng xué	Zài jiàn	Lǎo shī	Hǎo
Classmates	Good bye	Teacher	Good

同	你	好	我	老
学	好	再	叫	师
好	你	见	你	好

同学们 好!
Tóng xué men hǎo!
Hello classmates!

再见!
Zài jiàn!
Good bye!

再见 ♥

Did you know?
再见! also means "See you again!".

Match

Draw a line from each Chinese phrase to it's picture.

你好!
Nǐ hǎo
Hello!

再见!
Zài jiàn!
Good bye!

老师好!
Lǎo shī hǎo!
Hello teacher!

我叫
Wǒ jiào
My name is

HELLO
my name is
猫 Cat
Māo

你叫什么名字?
Nǐ jiào shén me míng zì?
What is your name?

同学们好!
Tóng xué men hǎo!
Hello classmates!

Vocabulary

Trace and write.   Follow the numbers to trace.

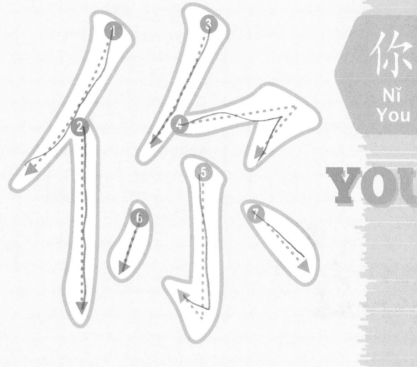

你
Nǐ
You

YOU

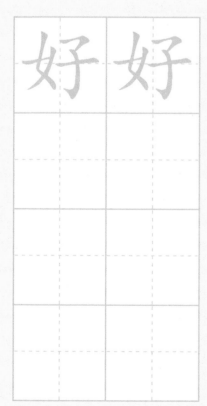

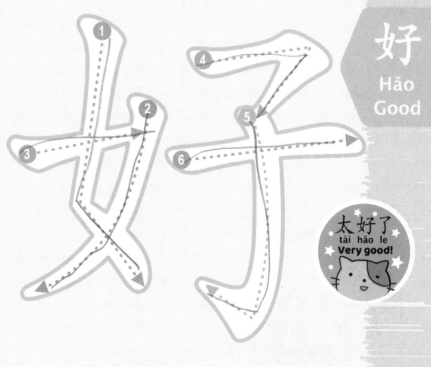

好
Hǎo
Good

太好了
tài hǎo le
Very good!

Vocabulary

Follow the numbers to trace.

Trace and write.

同
Tóng
With

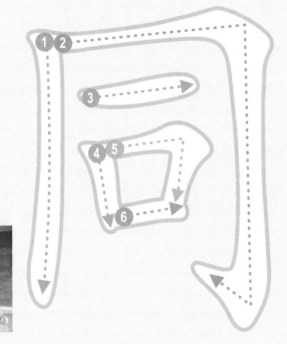

学
Xué
Learn

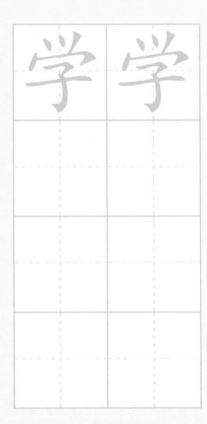

Vocabulary

Trace and write.   Follow the numbers to trace.

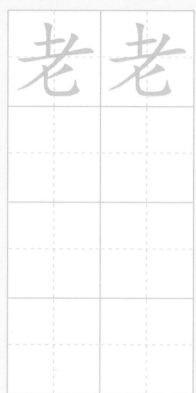

老
Lǎo
Old

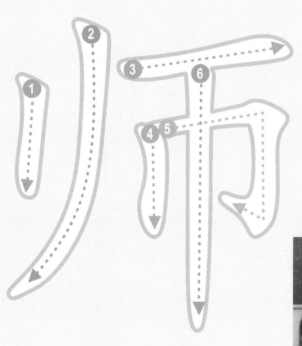

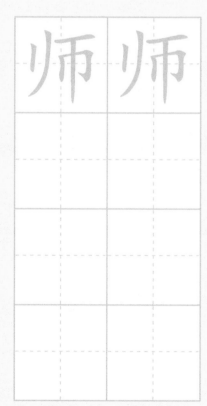

师
Shī
Expert

Vocabulary

Follow the numbers to trace.

Trace and write.

再
Zài
Again

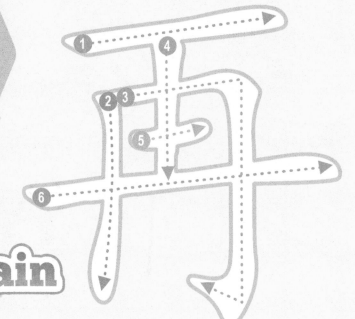

again

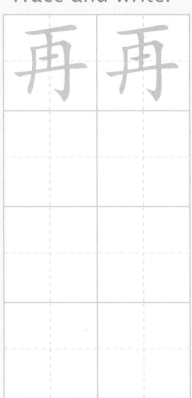

见
Jiàn
See

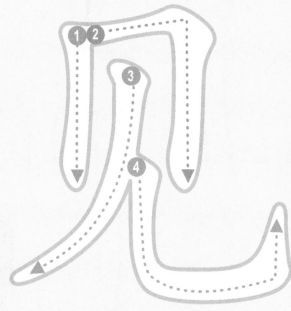

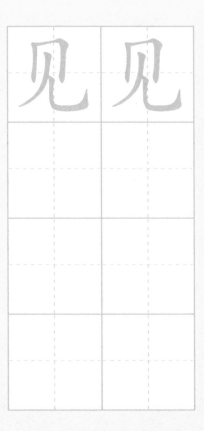

Vocabulary

Trace and write.

Follow the numbers to trace.

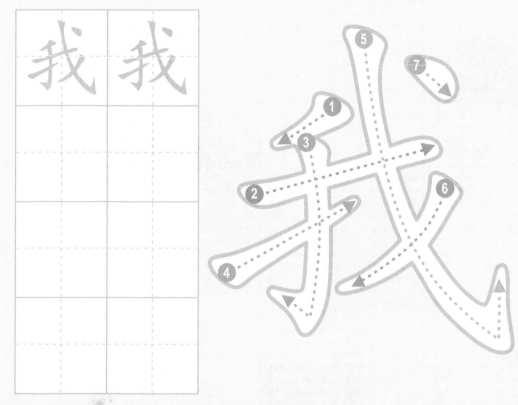

我
Wǒ
My, I, me

Draw a picture of how you feel today.

Be the Teacher!

Take turns being the teacher with these phrases.

请看。
Qǐng kàn
Please look.

注意听。
Zhù yì tīng
Listen carefully.

坐下。
Zuò xià
Sit down.

站起来。
Zhàn qǐ lái
Stand up.

请举手。
Qǐng jǔ shǒu
Please raise your hand.

Teacher's Day!

China, Taiwan and Singapore celebrate Teacher's Day in September. Teachers receive flowers as gifts.

Follow the words to reach the flower.

教师节!
Jiào shī jié!
Teacher's Day!

教师
Jiào shī

老师
Lǎo shī

教师
Jiào shī

老师
Lǎo shī

老师
Lǎo shī

教师
Jiào shī

Celebrate Teachers

Pick any day as Teacher's Day.
How will you celebrate?

教师
Jiào shī
School
Teacher

老师
Lǎo shī
Teacher

Match

Draw a line from each picture to its Chinese phrase.

站起来。
Zhàn qǐ lái
Stand up.

请看。
Qǐng kàn
Please look.

注意听。
Zhù yì tīng
Listen carefully.

坐下。
Zuò xià
Sit down.

请举手。
Qǐng jǔ shǒu
Please raise your hand.

Vocabulary

Trace and write.   Follow the numbers to trace.

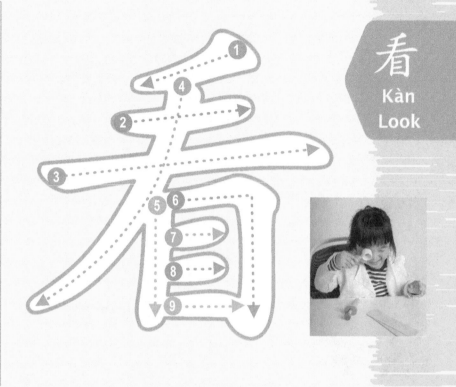

看
Kàn
Look

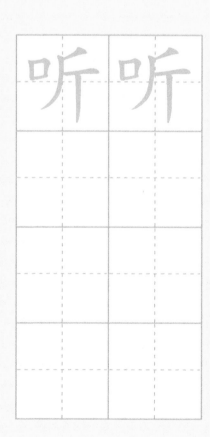

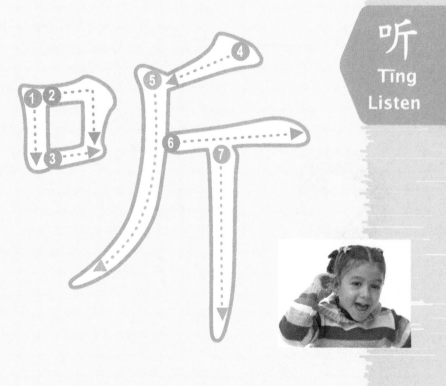

听
Tīng
Listen

Vocabulary

Follow the numbers to trace.

Trace and write.

坐
Zuò
Sit

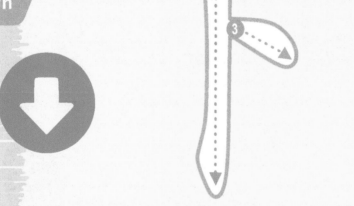

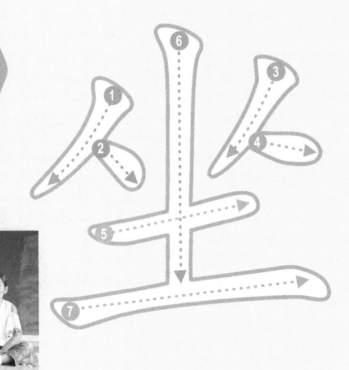

下
Xià
Down

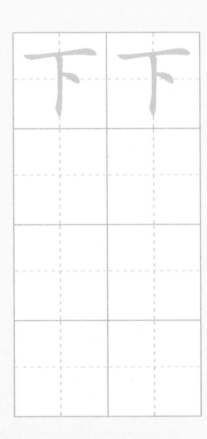

Vocabulary

Trace and write.   Follow the numbers to trace.

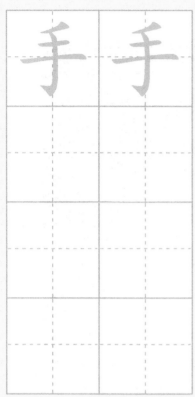

手
Shǒu
Hand

Draw what you think the girl is looking at.

请看
Qǐng kàn
Please look

Meet Confucius

Confucius taught his students to treat others the way they would like to be treated themselves.

孔子
Kǒng zǐ
Confucius

Who is Confucius?

Confucius is the most famous teacher in China's history. His teachings are known around the world.

Confucius was born in Qufu, China. This relic shows some of his teachings.

Chinese Proverbs

Confucius wrote many proverbs. Some proverbs or advice encouraged students to be kind.

谚语
Yàn yǔ
Proverb

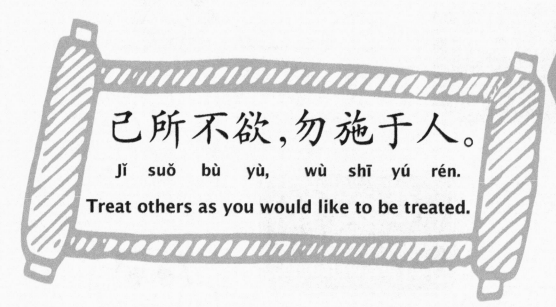

己所不欲，勿施于人。

Jǐ suǒ bù yù,   wù shī yú rén.

Treat others as you would like to be treated.

I Can Show Kindness By

Draw or write about how you can show kindness to others.

Be Kind

Take turns being kind to each other.

谢谢。
Xiè xiè
Thank you.

Thank you

不客气。
Bù kè qì
You are welcome.

You are welcome

Sorry

对不起。
Duì bù qǐ
Sorry.

没关系。
Méi guān xì
It's okay.

It's okay

Color each phrase.

谢谢
Thank you

不客气
You are welcome

对不起
Sorry

没关系
It's okay

Word Search

Find and circle these Chinese phrases in the heart.

谢谢。 Xiè xiè Thank you.	不客气。 Bù kè qì You are welcome.	对不起。 Duì bù qǐ Sorry.	没关系。 Méi guān xì It's okay.

Sorry 对不起　　It's okay 没关系

Thank 谢谢 you　　Sorry 对不起

You 不客气 are welcome

You are 不客气 welcome

谢谢 Thank you

It's okay 没关系

Match

Draw a line from each Chinese phrase to its English meaning.

不客气。
Bù kè qì

对不起。
Duì bù qǐ

You are welcome

Sorry   It's okay

Thank you

谢谢。
Xiè xiè

没关系。
Méi guān xì

Numbers

Learn numbers in Chinese from 1 to 10.

一
yī
one

二
èr
two

三
sān
three

四
sì
four

Try This!

Say the numbers in Chinese. Show how many using your fingers just like in the pictures.

五
wǔ
five

6

六
liù
six

1 to 99

For numbers 1 to 99, you only need to know how to write numbers in Chinese from 1 to 10.

7

七
qī
seven

8

八
bā
eight

9

九
jiǔ
nine

10

十
shí
ten

Match

Draw a line from each Chinese number to its matching picture.

一
yī
one

二
èr
two

三
sān
three

四
sì
four

五
wǔ
five

Match

Draw a line from each Chinese number to its matching picture.

六
liù
six

7

七
qī
seven

9

八
bā
eight

6

九
jiǔ
nine

8

十
shí
ten

10

Vocabulary

Follow the numbers to trace.

Trace and write.

一
yī
one

①

星星
Xīng xīng
Star

Color the number of star shapes.

一
yī
one

Vocabulary

二
èr
two

Trace and write.

Follow the numbers to trace.

二
èr
two

Color the number of bear shapes.

熊
Xióng
Bear

Vocabulary

Follow the numbers to trace.

Trace and write.

三
sān
three

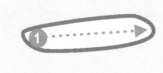

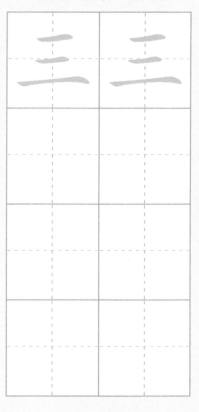

鸟
Niǎo
Bird

Color the number of bird shapes.

三
sān
three

Vocabulary

四
sì
four

Trace and write.

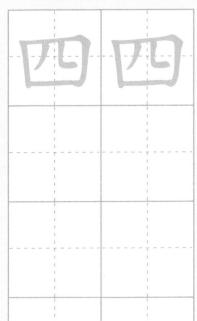

Follow the numbers to trace.

四
sì
four

Color the number of rabbit shapes.

兔子
Tù zǐ
Rabbit

Vocabulary

Follow the numbers to trace.

Trace and write.

五
wǔ
five

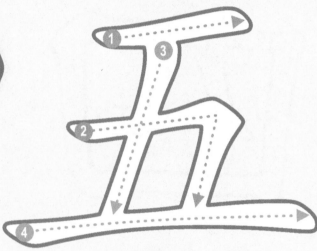

五 五

Color the number of flower shapes.

花
Huā
Flower

五
wǔ
five

Vocabulary

Trace and write.   Follow the numbers to trace.

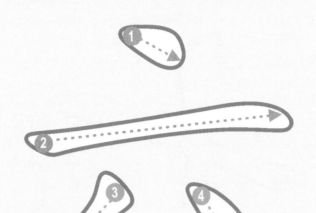

六
liù
six

Color the number of star shapes.

六
liù
six

星星
Xīng xīng
Star

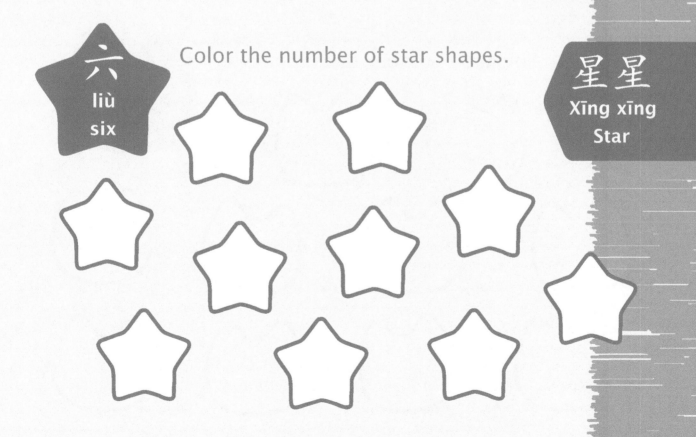

Vocabulary

Follow the numbers to trace.

Trace and write.

七
qī
seven

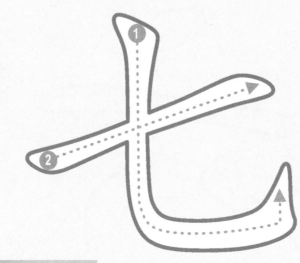

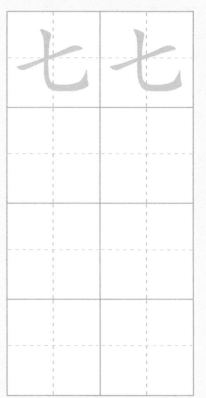

7

猫
Māo
Cat

Color the number of cat shapes.

七
qī
seven

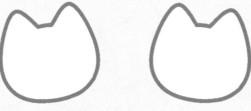

Vocabulary

Trace and write.

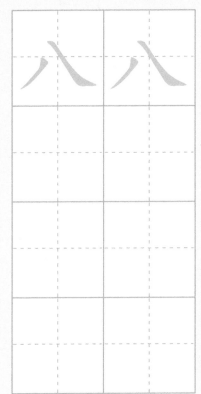

Follow the numbers to trace.

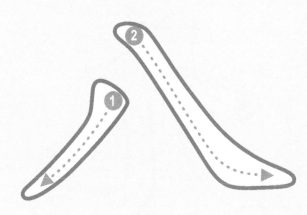

bā
eight

Color the number of flower shapes.

Vocabulary

九
jiǔ
nine

Follow the numbers to trace.

Trace and write.

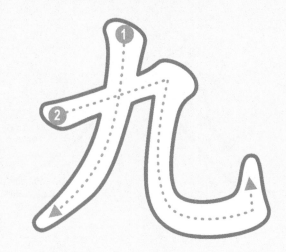

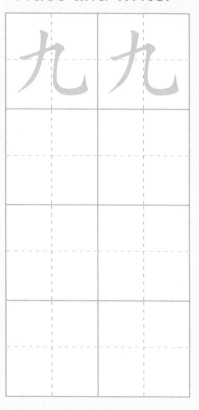

花
Huā
Flower

Color the number of flower shapes.

九
jiǔ
nine

Vocabulary

Trace and write.   Follow the numbers to trace.

Color the number of star shapes.

Find and Color

Find and color the parts with Chinese characters.

一 yī one

二 èr two

三 sān three

四 sì four

五 wǔ five

六 liù six

七 qī seven

八 bā eight

九 jiǔ nine

十 shí ten

Dot to Dot

Help complete the drawing.
Draw a line to connect the dots from 一 to 十.
Draw your own cover.

书
Shū
Book

一
yī
one

二
èr
two

三
sān
three

四
sì
four

五
wǔ
five

六
liù
six

七
qī
seven

八
bā
eight

九
jiǔ
nine

十
shí
ten

Numbers

Numbers in Chinese from 11 to 19 begin with 十 (shí).

Pattern

Look at the numbers in each train. Do you see a pattern?

Trace the numbers in Chinese.

10　十

6　六

16　十 六
shí liù

10　十

7　七

17　十 七
shí qī

10　十

8　八

18　十 八
shí bā

10　十

9　九

19　十 九
shí jiǔ

火车
Huǒ chē
Train

To write numbers 11 to 19,
use 十 (shí) with a number
from 一 (yī) to 九 (jiǔ).

Numbers

Numbers in Chinese from 20 to 29 begin with 二 (èr) and 十 (shí).

Pattern

Look at the numbers in each train. Do you see a pattern?

2	10	20
二 èr	十 shí	二十 èr shí

2	10	1	21
二 èr	十 shí	一 yī	二十一 èr shí yī

2	10	2	22
二 èr	十 shí	二 èr	二十二 èr shí èr

2	10	3	23
二 èr	十 shí	三 sān	二十三 èr shí sān

2	10	4	24
二 èr	十 shí	四 sì	二十四 èr shí sì

To write numbers 21 to 29, use 二 (èr) and 十 (shí) with a number from 一 (yī) to 九 (jiǔ).

Trace the numbers in Chinese.

2	10	5	25
二	十	五	二十五 èr shí wǔ
2	10	6	26
二	十	六	二十六 èr shí liù
2	10	7	27
二	十	七	二十七 èr shí qī
2	10	8	28
二	十	八	二十八 èr shí bā
2	10	9	29
二	十	九	二十九 èr shí jiǔ

Numbers

Numbers in Chinese from 30 to 39 begin with 三 (sān) and 十 (shí).

Pattern

Look at the numbers in each train. Do you see a pattern?

3	10	30
三 sān	十 shí	三十 sān shí

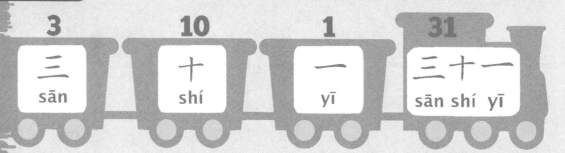

3	10	1	31
三 sān	十 shí	一 yī	三十一 sān shí yī

3	10	2	32
三 sān	十 shí	二 èr	三十二 sān shí èr

3	10	3	33
三 sān	十 shí	三 sān	三十三 sān shí sān

3	10	4	34
三 sān	十 shí	四 sì	三十四 sān shí sì

To write numbers 31 to 39, use 三 (sān) and 十 (shí) with a number from 一 (yī) to 九 (jiǔ).

Trace the numbers in Chinese.

3   10   5   35
三 十 五   三十五 sān shí wǔ

3   10   6   36
三 十 六   三十六 sān shí liù

Write the numbers in Chinese.

3   10   7   37
三十七 sān shí qī

3   10   8   38
三十八 sān shí bā

3   10   9   39
三十九 sān shí jiǔ

Numbers

Numbers in Chinese from 40 to 49 begin with 四 (sì) and 十 (shí).

Pattern

Look at the numbers in each train. Do you see a pattern?

4 四 sì   **10** 十 shí   **40** 四十 sì shí

4 四 sì   **10** 十 shí   **1** 一 yī   **41** 四十一 sì shí yī

4 四 sì   **10** 十 shí   **2** 二 èr   **42** 四十二 sì shí èr

4 四 sì   **10** 十 shí   **3** 三 sān   **43** 四十三 sì shí sān

4 四 sì   **10** 十 shí   **4** 四 sì   **44** 四十四 sì shí sì

To write numbers 41 to 49, use 四 (sì) and 十 (shí) with a number from 一 (yī) to 九 (jiǔ).

Trace the numbers in Chinese.

4	10	5	45
四	十	五	四十五 sì shí wǔ

4	10	6	46
四	十	六	四十六 sì shí liù

Write the numbers in Chinese.

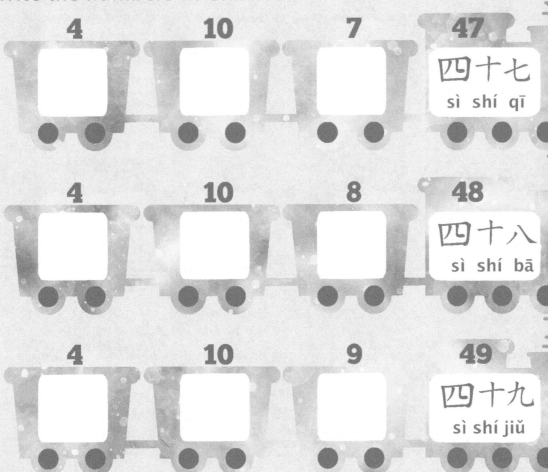

4	10	7	47
			四十七 sì shí qī

4	10	8	48
			四十八 sì shí bā

4	10	9	49
			四十九 sì shí jiǔ

Numbers

Numbers in Chinese from 50 to 59 begin with
五 (wǔ) and 十 (shí).

Pattern

Look at the
numbers in each
train. Do you
see a pattern?

5 五 wǔ   **10** 十 shí   **50** 五十 wǔ shí

5 五 wǔ   **10** 十 shí   **1** 一 yī   **51** 五十一 wǔ shí yī

5 五 wǔ   **10** 十 shí   **2** 二 èr   **52** 五十二 wǔ shí èr

5 五 wǔ   **10** 十 shí   **3** 三 sān   **53** 五十三 wǔ shí sān

5 五 wǔ   **10** 十 shí   **4** 四 sì   **54** 五十四 wǔ shí sì

To write numbers 51 to 59, use 五 (wǔ) and 十 (shí) with a number from 一 (yī) to 九 (jiǔ).

Trace the numbers in Chinese.

5 五 **10** 十 **5** 五 **55** 五十五 wǔ shí wǔ

5 五 **10** 十 **6** 六 **56** 五十六 wǔ shí liù

Write the numbers in Chinese.

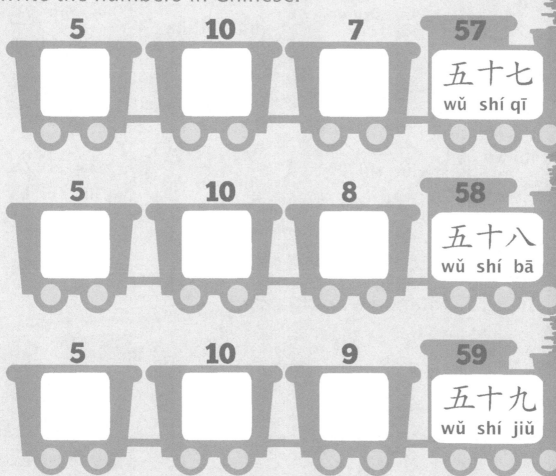

5 **10** **7** **57** 五十七 wǔ shí qī

5 **10** **8** **58** 五十八 wǔ shí bā

5 **10** **9** **59** 五十九 wǔ shí jiǔ

Numbers

Numbers in Chinese from 60 to 69 begin with 六 (liù) and 十 (shí).

6	10	60
六 liù	十 shí	六 十 liù shí

To write numbers 61 to 69, use 六 (liù) and 十 (shí) with a number from 一 (yī) to 九 (jiǔ).

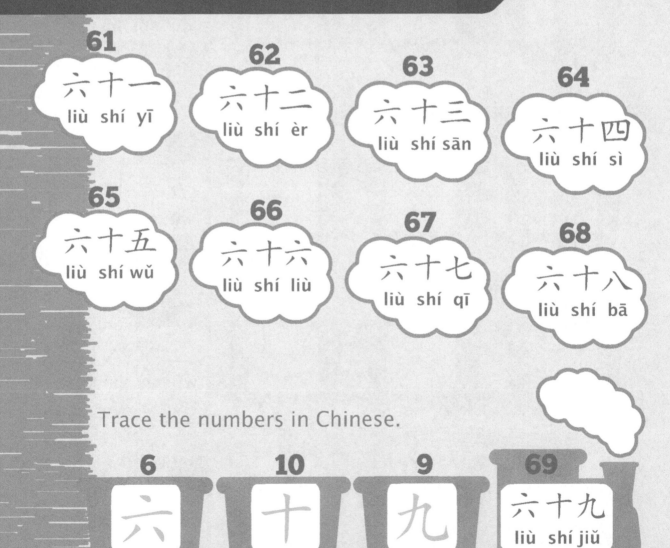

61
六 十 一
liù shí yī

62
六 十 二
liù shí èr

63
六 十 三
liù shí sān

64
六 十 四
liù shí sì

65
六 十 五
liù shí wǔ

66
六 十 六
liù shí liù

67
六 十 七
liù shí qī

68
六 十 八
liù shí bā

Trace the numbers in Chinese.

6	10	9	69
六	十	九	六 十 九 liù shí jiǔ

Numbers

Numbers in Chinese from 70 to 79 begin with 七 (qī) and 十 (shí).

7	10	70
七 qī	十 shí	七 十 qī shí

To write numbers 71 to 79, use 七 (qī) and 十 (shí) with a number from 一 (yī) to 九 (jiǔ).

71
七 十 一
qī shí yī

72
七 十 二
qī shí èr

73
七 十 三
qī shí sān

74
七 十 四
qī shí sì

75
七 十 五
qī shí wǔ

76
七 十 六
qī shí liù

77
七 十 七
qī shí qī

78
七 十 八
qī shí bā

Trace the numbers in Chinese.

7	10	9	79
七	十	九	七 十 九 qī shí jiǔ

Numbers

Numbers in Chinese from 80 to 89 begin with 八 (bā) and 十 (shí).

8	10	80
八 bā	十 shí	八 十 bā shí

To write numbers 81 to 89, use 八 (bā) and 十 (shí) with a number from 一 (yī) to 九 (jiǔ).

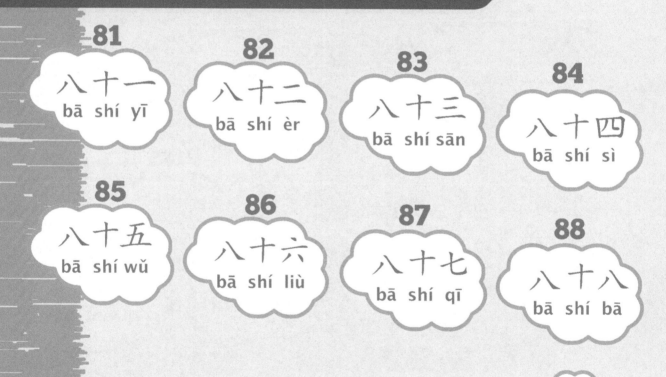

81
八 十 一
bā shí yī

82
八 十 二
bā shí èr

83
八 十 三
bā shí sān

84
八 十 四
bā shí sì

85
八 十 五
bā shí wǔ

86
八 十 六
bā shí liù

87
八 十 七
bā shí qī

88
八 十 八
bā shí bā

Trace the numbers in Chinese.

8	10	9	89
八	十	九	八 十 九 bā shí jiǔ

Numbers

Numbers in Chinese from 90 to 99 begin with
九 (jiǔ) and 十 (shí).

9
九
jiǔ

10
十
shí

90
九十
qī shí

To write numbers 91 to 99, use 九 (jiǔ) and 十 (shí)
with a number from 一 (yī) to 九 (jiǔ).

91
九十一
jiǔ shí yī

92
九十二
jiǔ shí èr

93
九十三
jiǔ shí sān

94
九十四
jiǔ shí sì

95
九十五
jiǔ shí wǔ

96
九十六
jiǔ shí liù

97
九十七
jiǔ shí qī

98
九十八
jiǔ shí bā

Trace the numbers in Chinese.

9
九

10
十

9
九

99
九十九
jiǔ shí jiǔ

Photo Puzzle

Draw a line from each missing piece to where it belongs in the picture.

火车
Huǒ chē
Train

Hint: The whole train picture is on page 42.

Vocabulary

Trace and write.

Follow the numbers to trace.

火
huǒ
fire

Trace and write.

Follow the numbers to trace.

车
chē
car

Animals

How do animals sound in Chinese?

咩
miē

羊
Yáng
Sheep

叽
jī

鸟
Niǎo
Bird

汪
wāng

狗
Gǒu
Dog

咯
gē

鸡
Jī
Chicken

Try This!

Pretend to be an animal by making its sounds in Chinese. Who can guess which animal you are?

猫
Māo
Cat

喵
miāo

Measure Word

A measure word is used in between the number and noun (person, place, animal or thing) to show one or more of that noun.

只 (zhī) is used for counting most animals (except large animals and those with long bodies).

一只羊
Yī   zhī   yáng
One sheep

一只鸟
Yī   zhī   niǎo
One bird

只
zhī
measure
word

Trace and write.

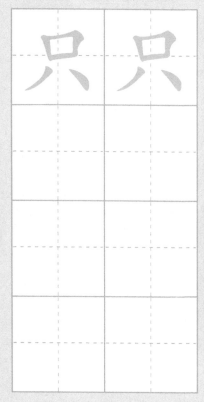

Follow the numbers to trace.

Counting Tip

Use the same noun for one or more than one. To show how many, use

Number + Measure word + Noun

Counting Two

A different word for the number 2 is used when there is a total of two things, animals or people (not for pairs).

两
Liǎng
Two

有几只羊?
Yǒu jǐ zhī yáng?
How many sheep?

两只羊。
Liǎng zhī yáng
Two sheep.

一只羊
Yī zhī yáng
One sheep

两只羊
Liǎng zhī yáng
Two sheep

一
Yī
One

二
Èr
Two

Counting Tip

两 (liǎng) must be used with a measure word.

Vocabulary

两
Liǎng
Two

Trace and write.   Follow the numbers to trace.

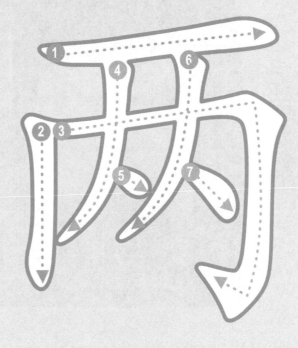

Trace the Chinese characters.

Two cats.
Liǎng   zhī   māo.

两 只 猫 。

Two birds.
Liǎng   zhī   niǎo.

两 只 鸟 。

Sheep

Take turns asking who has sheep.

你有羊吗？
Nǐ yǒu yáng ma?
Do you have sheep?

我有羊。
Wǒ yǒu yáng.
I have sheep.

我没有羊。
Wǒ méi yǒu yáng.
I don't have sheep.

Draw sheep 羊 (yáng) in the meadow.

Vocabulary

Trace and write.   Follow the numbers to trace.

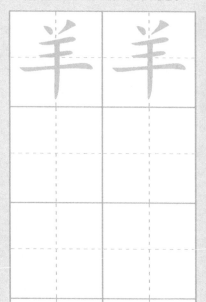

羊
Yáng
Sheep

有几只羊?
Yǒu jǐ zhī yáng?
How many sheep?

Count in Chinese.
Color the number of squares.

五只羊。
Wǔ zhī yáng
Five sheep.

Birds

Take turns asking who has birds.

我有鸟。
Wǒ yǒu niǎo.
I have birds.

你有鸟吗?
Nǐ yǒu niǎo ma?
Do you have birds?

我没有鸟。
Wǒ méi yǒu niǎo.
I don't have birds.

Draw birds 鸟 (niǎo) in the forest.

Vocabulary

Trace and write.

Follow the numbers to trace.

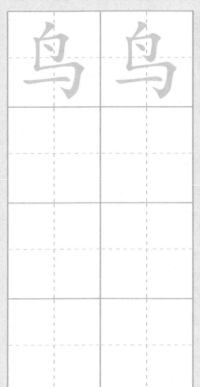

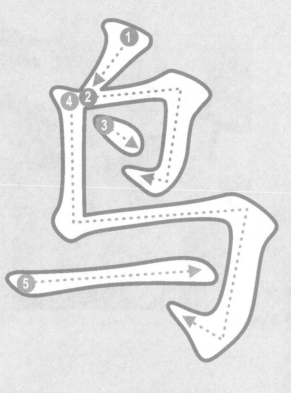

鸟
Niǎo
Bird(s)

有几只鸟?
Yǒu jǐ zhī niǎo?
How many birds?

Count in Chinese.
Color the number of squares.

三只鸟。
Sān zhī niǎo
Three birds.

Dogs

Take turns asking who has dogs.

我有狗。
Wǒ yǒu gǒu.
I have dogs.

你有狗吗?
Nǐ yǒu gǒu ma?
Do you have dogs?

我没有狗。
Wǒ méi yǒu gǒu.
I don't have dogs.

Draw dogs 狗 (gǒu) in the orchard.

Vocabulary

Trace and write.   Follow the numbers to trace.

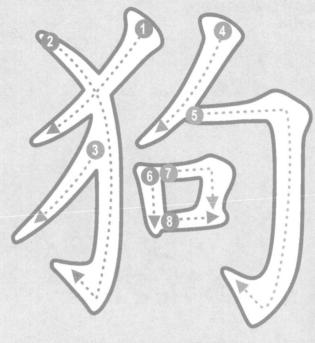

狗
Gǒu
Dog(s)

有几只狗?
Yǒu jǐ zhī gǒu?
How many dogs?

Count in Chinese.
Color the number of squares.

四只狗。
Sì zhī gǒu
Four dogs.

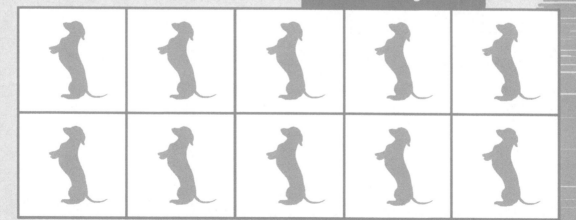

Cats

Take turns asking who has cats.

你有猫吗?

Nǐ yǒu māo ma?

Do you have cats?

我有猫。

Wǒ yǒu māo.

I have cats.

我没有猫。

Wǒ méi yǒu māo.

I don't have cats.

Draw cats 猫 (māo) on the grass.

Vocabulary

Trace and write.   Follow the numbers to trace.

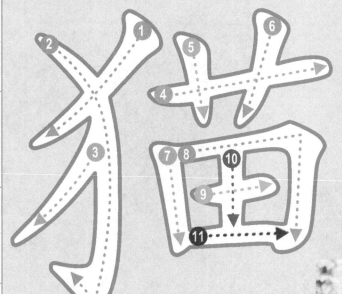

猫
Māo
Cat(s)

有几只猫?
Yǒu jǐ zhī māo?
How many cats?

Count in Chinese.
Color the number of squares.

八只猫。
Bā zhī māo
Eight cats.

Chicken

Take turns asking who has chickens.

我有鸡。
Wǒ yǒu jī.
I have chickens.

你有鸡吗?
Nǐ yǒu jī ma?
Do you have chickens?

我没有鸡。
Wǒ méi yǒu jī.
I don't have chickens.

Draw chickens 鸡 (jī) in the field.

Vocabulary

Trace and write.   Follow the numbers to trace.

鸡
Jī
Chicken(s)

有几只鸡？
Yǒu jǐ zhī jī?
How many chickens?

Count in Chinese.
Color the number of squares.

九只鸡。
Jiǔ zhī jī
Nine chickens.

Vocabulary

有
Yǒu
Have

没
Méi
No

Trace and write.

Follow the numbers to trace.

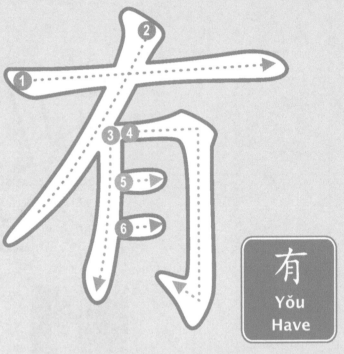

有
Yǒu
Have

Trace and write.

Follow the numbers to trace.

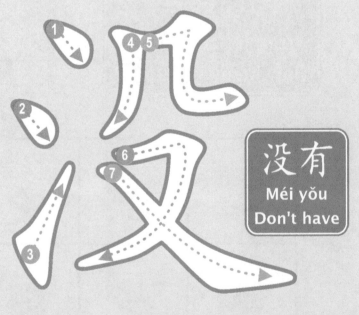

没有
Méi yǒu
Don't have

Silly Game

Circle the correct choice for each question.

Do sheep have wings?

有
Yǒu
Have

没有
Méi yǒu
Don't have

Do birds have beaks?

有
Yǒu
Have

没有
Méi yǒu
Don't have

Do dogs have tails?

有
Yǒu
Have

没有
Méi yǒu
Don't have

Lucky Dog

If a dog goes to a house and is invited inside, it will bring good luck.

Do chickens have wool?

有
Yǒu
Have

没有
Méi yǒu
Don't have

Do cats have feathers?

有
Yǒu
Have

没有
Méi yǒu
Don't have

Family Time

Let's meet family members in Chinese.

Dad's Parents

Mom's Parents

爷爷
Yé ye
Grandpa

外公
Wài gōng
Grandpa

奶奶
Nǎi nai
Grandma

家
Jiā
Family

外婆
Wài pó
Grandma

爸爸
Bà ba
Dad

妈妈
Mā ma
Mom

姐姐
Jiě jie
Older Sister

哥哥
Gē ge
Older Brother

妹妹
Mèi mei
Younger Sister

弟弟
Dì di
Younger Brother

Vocabulary

Trace and write.

Follow the numbers to trace.

爷爷
Yé ye
Grandpa
(Dad's side)

Trace and write.

Follow the numbers to trace.

奶奶
Nǎi nai
Grandma
(Dad's side)

Vocabulary

外公
Wài gōng
Grandpa (Mom's side)

Trace and write.

Follow the numbers to trace.

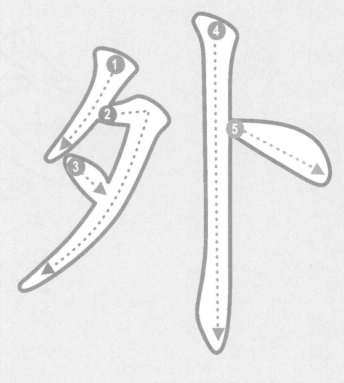

Trace and write.

Follow the numbers to trace.

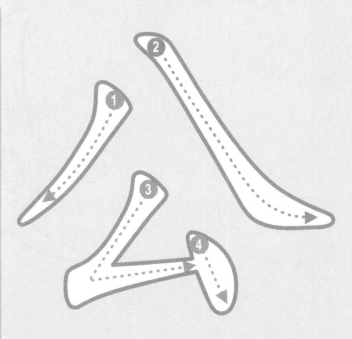

Vocabulary

Trace and write.

Follow the numbers to trace.

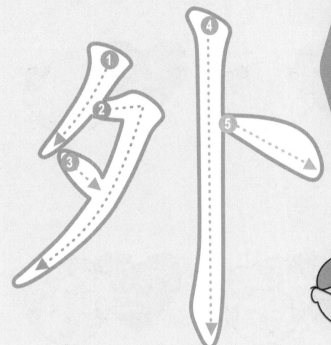

外婆
Wài pó
Grandma
(Mom's
side)

Trace and write.

Follow the numbers to trace.

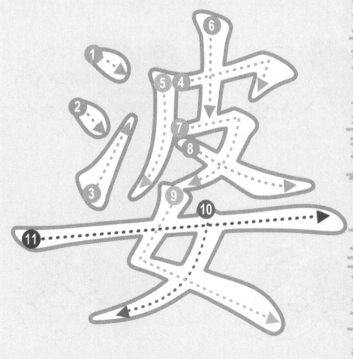

I Spy Game

Circle who is different in each row.

Vocabulary

Trace and write.

Follow the numbers to trace.

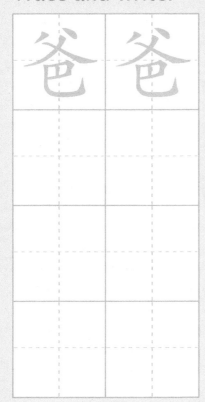

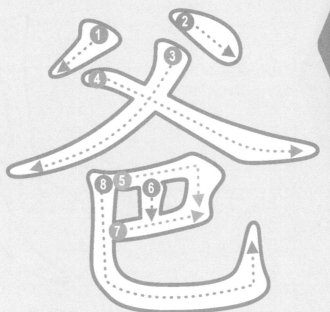

爸爸
Bà ba
Dad

Trace and write.

Follow the numbers to trace.

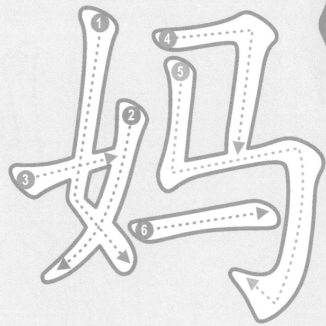

妈妈
Mā ma
Mom

Vocabulary

姐姐
Jiě jie
Older
Sister

Trace and write.

姐	姐

Follow the numbers to trace.

妹妹
Mèi mei
Younger
Sister

Trace and write.

妹	妹

Follow the numbers to trace.

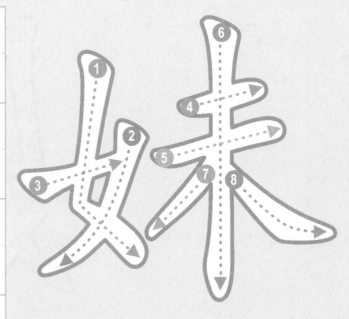

Vocabulary

Trace and write.

Follow the numbers to trace.

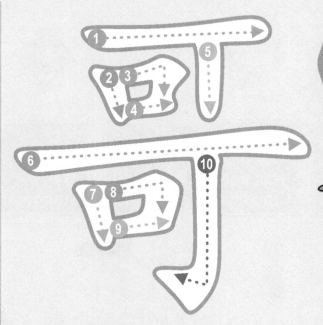

哥哥
Gē ge
Older Brother

Trace and write.

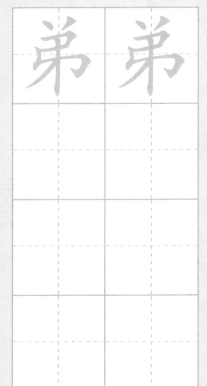

Follow the numbers to trace.

弟弟
Dì di
Younger Brother

Hide and Seek

Can you find all the family members?

爷爷	奶奶	外公	外婆	爸爸	妈妈
Yé ye	Nǎi nai	Wài gōng	Wài pó	Bà ba	Mā ma
Grandpa	Grandma	Grandpa	Grandma	Dad	Mom

家人
Jiā rén
Family member(s)

哥哥	姐姐	弟弟	妹妹
Gē ge	Jiě jie	Dì di	Mèi mei
Older Brother	Older Sister	Younger Brother	Younger Sister

I Love My Family

我爱我的家。
Wǒ ài wǒ de jiā.
I love my family.

Dad's Parents

我爱我的爷爷。
Wǒ ài wǒ de yé ye.
I love my grandpa.

我爱我的奶奶。
Wǒ ài wǒ de nǎi nai.
I love my grandma.

Mom's Parents

我爱我的外公。
Wǒ ài wǒ de wài gōng.
I love my grandpa.

我爱我的外婆。
Wǒ ài wǒ de wài pó.
I love my grandma.

My Parents

我爱我的爸爸。
Wǒ ài wǒ de bà ba.
I love my dad.

我爱我的妈妈。
Wǒ ài wǒ de mā ma.
I love my mom.

我爱我的哥哥。
Wǒ ài wǒ de gē ge.
I love my older brother.

我爱我的姐姐。
Wǒ ài wǒ de jiě jie.
I love my older sister.

我爱我的弟弟。
Wǒ ài wǒ de dì di.
I love my younger brother.

我爱我的妹妹。
Wǒ ài wǒ de mèi mei.
I love my younger sister.

我爱我自己。
Wǒ ài wǒ zì jǐ.
I love myself.

Draw a picture of you.

我爱我自己。
Wǒ ài wǒ zì jǐ.
I love myself.

Who Is This?

Draw a line from each face to its matching shape.

这是谁?
Zhè shì shuí?
Who is this?

Dad's Parents

这是爷爷。
Zhè shì yé ye.
This is grandpa.

这是奶奶。
Zhè shì nǎi nai.
This is grandma.

Mom's Parents

这是外公。
Zhè shì wài gōng.
This is grandpa.

这是外婆。
Zhè shì wài pó.
This is grandma.

This is

Draw a line from each face to its matching shape.

这是
Zhè shì
This is

这是爸爸。
Zhè shì bà ba.
This is dad.

这是妈妈。
Zhè shì mā ma.
This is mom.

这是哥哥。
Zhè shì gē ge.
This is older brother.

这是姐姐。
Zhè shì jiě jie.
This is older sister.

这是弟弟。
Zhè shì dì di.
This is younger brother.

这是妹妹。
Zhè shì mèi mei.
This is younger sister.

Your Family

Let's meet members of your family.

Draw a picture of you.

这就是我。
Zhè jiù shì wǒ.
This is me.

这是
Zhè shì
This is

Draw a picture of each person in your family.
Use the phrase 这是 to introduce each member in Chinese.

这是
Zhè shì
This is

Vocabulary

Trace and write.

Follow the numbers to trace.

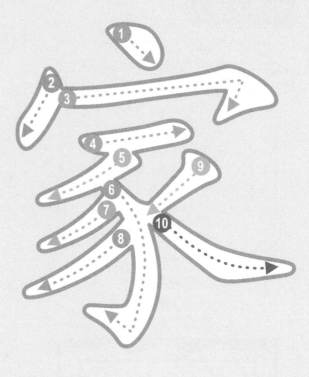

Trace and write.

Follow the numbers to trace.

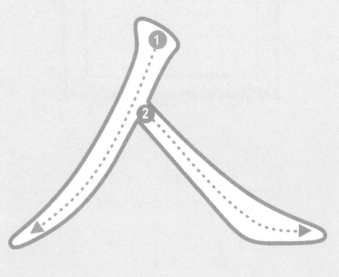

Vocabulary

Trace and write.   Follow the numbers to trace.

爱
Ài
Love

Draw the other side of the heart.

I Love You
Trace the Chinese characters.

我 爱 你。
Wǒ ài nǐ.
I love you.

Grandpa, I love you. Dad's Parent
Yé   ye   ,   wǒ   ài   nǐ   .

爷   爷   ，   我   爱   你   。
74   74   12   90   8

Grandma, I love you. Dad's Parent
Nǎi   nai   ,   wǒ   ài   nǐ   .

奶   奶   ，   我   爱   你   。
74   74   12   90   8

Grandpa, I love you. Mom's Parent
Wài   gōng   ,   wǒ   ài   nǐ   .

外   公   ，   我   爱   你   。
75   75   12   90   8

Grandma, I love you. Mom's Parent
Wài   pó   ,   wǒ   ài   nǐ   .

外   婆   ，   我   爱   你   。
76   76   12   90   8

Hint: Look for a circle with the page number where you can find a writing diagram.

92

Dad, I love you.

Bà	ba		wǒ	ài	nǐ	
爸	爸	，	我	爱	你	○
78	78		12	90	8	

Mom, I love you.

Mā	ma		wǒ	ài	nǐ	
妈	妈	，	我	爱	你	○
78	78		12	90	8	

Older sister, I love you.

Jiě	jie		wǒ	ài	nǐ	
姐	姐	，	我	爱	你	○
79	79		12	90	8	

Younger sister, I love you.

Mèi	mei		wǒ	ài	nǐ	
妹	妹	，	我	爱	你	○
79	79		12	90	8	

I Love You

Trace the Chinese characters.

我 爱 你。
Wǒ ài nǐ.
I love you.

Older brother, I love you.

Gē	ge	,	wǒ	ài	nǐ	.
哥	哥	，	我	爱	你	○
80	80		12	90	8	

Younger brother, I love you.

Dì	di	,	wǒ	ài	nǐ	.
弟	弟	，	我	爱	你	○
80	80		12	90	8	

Did you know?

Children's Day is celebrated in China, Taiwan and Singapore. It is a holiday just for kids like you!

儿 童 节
Ér tóng jié
Children's Day

Try This!

Pick a date as Children's Day. Draw or write how you want to celebrate.

Writing Practice

Use this page to practice writing Chinese characters.
Try to write one row of characters each day.

Writing Practice

Use this page to practice writing Chinese characters
Try to write one row of characters each day.

干得好
gàn de hǎo
Well done!

Writing Practice

Use this page to practice writing Chinese characters.
Try to write one row of characters each day.

Writing Practice

Use this page to practice writing Chinese characters.
Try to write one row of characters each day.

Writing Practice

Use this page to practice writing Chinese characters.
Try to write one row of characters each day.

太棒了
tài bàng le
Awesome!

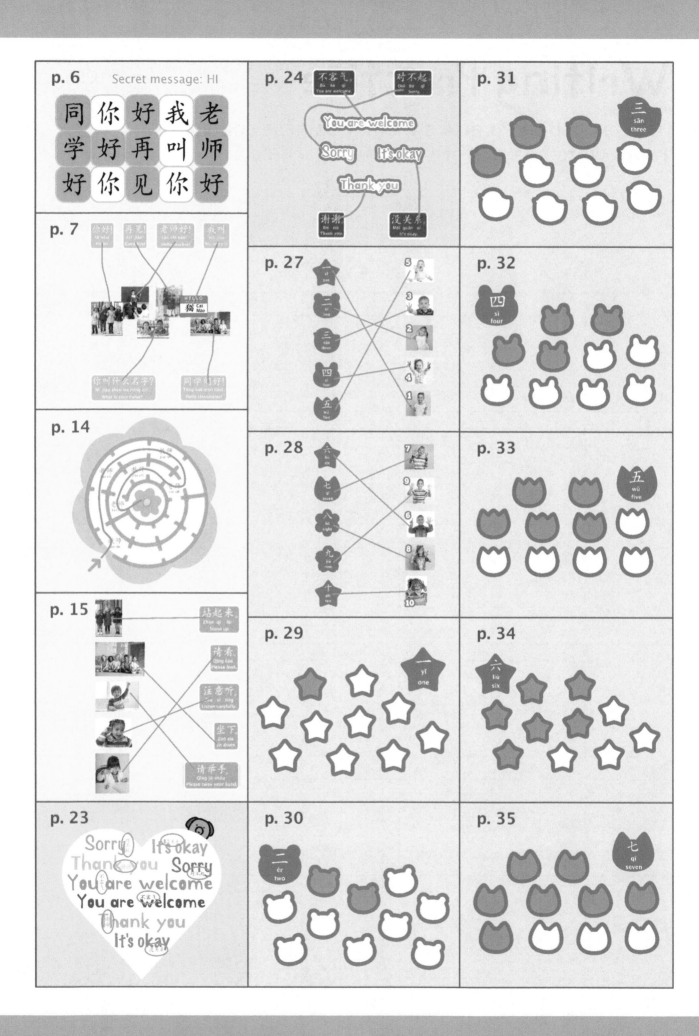

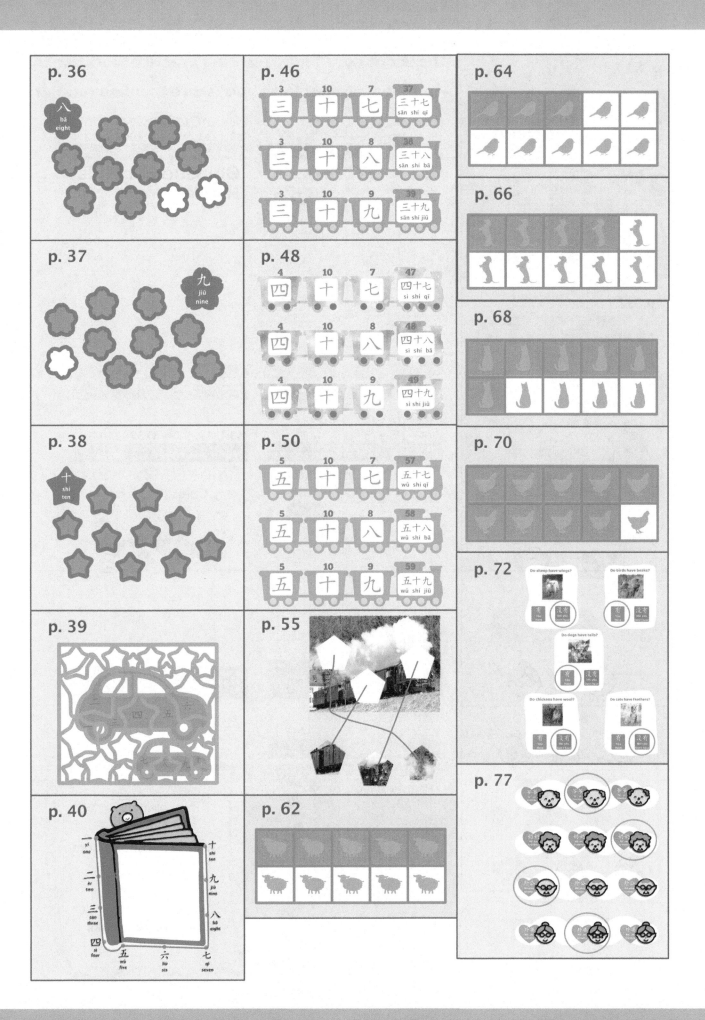

p. 81

p. 82

p. 85

p. 86

Check out our Chinese writing practice workbooks.
Find them at your local bookstore & online retailers.

ISBN-10: 1717734472
ISBN-13: 978-1717734471

Simplified Chinese Practice Writing Pages ages 5+

Chinese For Kids
First 50 Characters
头50个汉字(简体)

一 马 书 书
书 书 书 书
书 书 书 书

● Chinese character recognition through writing.
● Build child's confidence in writing Chinese.
● Develop early Chinese language writing skills.

ISBN-10: 1720475741
ISBN-13: 978-1720475743

Simplified Chinese Practice Writing Pages ages 5+

Chinese For Kids
50 More Characters
50多个汉字(简体)

丿 一 字
字 字 字 字
字 字 字 字

● Chinese character recognition through writing.
● Build child's confidence in writing Chinese.
● Develop early Chinese language writing skills.

ISBN-10: 1797428977
ISBN-13: 978-1797428970

Simplified Chinese Practice Writing Pages ages 4+

Chinese For Kids
First Practice Strokes

你好
山
吃
eat
chi

● Encourage pencil control with fun exercises.
● Build child's confidence in writing Chinese.
● Develop early Chinese language writing skills.

ISBN-13: 979-8737051440

Simplified Chinese Writing Practice ages 6+

Chinese For Kids
My Colors Workbook
我的颜色

Trace and write.

● Chinese character recognition through writing.
● Build child's confidence in writing Chinese.
● Develop early Chinese language writing skills.

ISBN-10: 1717734472
ISBN-13: 978-1717734471

Blank Practice Writing Pages With Grids ages 5+

Chinese For Kids
Practice Notebook
1 inch Grids Tian Zi Ge Cat Edition 猫

● 100 pages of blank practice pages with grids.
● Large grids with dashed lines to guide strokes.
● 35 grids on each page with whimsical cats.

http://

www.adoreneko.com

Instagram

@adorenekobooks